The Permanent Way

David Hare is one of Britain's most internationally
performed playwrights. Born in Sussex in 1947, he had
a long association with Britain's National Theatre, which
produced eleven of his plays successively between 1978
and 1997. A trilogy about the Church, the Law and the
Labour Party – *Racing Demon, Murmuring Judges* and
The Absence of War – was presented in repertory at the
Olivier Theatre in 1993. Nine of his best-known plays,
including *Plenty, The Secret Rapture, Skylight, The Blue
Room, Amy's View, The Judas Kiss* and *Via Dolorosa* –
in which he performed – have also been presented on
Broadway.

DAVID HARE

The Permanent Way

or

LA VOIE ANGLAISE

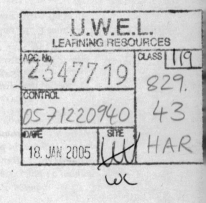

faber and faber

First published in 2003
by Faber and Faber Limited
3 Queen Square London WC1N 3AU
Published in the United States by Faber and Faber Inc.
an affiliate of Farrar, Straus and Giroux LLC, New York

Typeset by Country Setting, Kingsdown, Kent CT14 8ES
Printed in England by Mackays of Chatham plc, Chatham, Kent

David Hare is hereby identified as author
of this work in accordance with Section 77 of the
Copyright, Designs and Patents Act 1988

A CIP record for this book
is available from the British Library

ISBN 0–571–22094–0

2 4 6 8 10 9 7 5 3 1

Author's Note

I would like to thank everyone who contributed to the writing of this play. *The Permanent Way* was developed by the Out of Joint Theatre Company and started off with a workshop period at the National Theatre Studio. Early interviews were gathered with the help of nine actors – Nigel Cooke, Matthew Dunster, Lloyd Hutchinson, Paterson Joseph, Bella Merlin, Maxine Peake, Pearce Quigley, Sally Rogers and Peter Wight. The research period was expertly co-ordinated by Matthew Wilde.

In the months of work, we have had countless meetings with individuals and experts to whom I am indebted for their generosity with their time, their knowledge and their experience. Only a fraction of them are directly represented. There is also a lot of good writing about the railways, but I am especially grateful to Ian Jack for his 90-page gem, *The Crash that Stopped Britain* (Granta Books).

The play is updated during its run.

The Permanent Way was first presented at the Theatre
Royal, York, on 13 November 2003, in a co-production
between Out of Joint and the National Theatre. It opened
in the Cottesloe auditorium of the National Theatre,
London, on 6 January 2004, with the following cast:

Flaminia Cinque
Nigel Cooke
Matthew Dunster
Souad Faress
Sam Graham
Lloyd Hutchinson
Kika Markham
Bella Merlin
Ian Redford

Director Max Stafford-Clark
Designer William Dudley
Lighting Designer Johanna Town
Sound Designer Paul Arditti
Costume Supervisor Hattie Barsby
Assistant Director Naomi Jones
Researcher Matthew Wilde

Characters

A High-Powered Treasury Thinker
A Senior Civil Servant
An Investment Banker
Wendy
John Prescott
A Very Experienced Rail Engineer
A Senior Rail Executive
Sally
A Leading Entrepreneur
Catweasel
Rocker
Rustin' Hoffman
Big Heap
Sven
Stormin' Norman
Piemuncher
JH
Doghole
A British Transport Policeman
A Bereaved Mother
A Bereaved Father
A Rail Union Leader
An Assistant General Secretary
Dawn
A Campaigning Solicitor
A Young Man in Denim
A Second Bereaved Mother
A Survivors' Group Founder
A Managing Director of Railtrack
Lord Cullen

Another Senior Operating Executive
A Vicar of Hatfield
A Scottish Literary Editor
A Technical Director of a Maintenance Company
A Squadron Leader
A Bereaved Widow

Passengers, Lawyers, etc.

THE PERMANENT WAY

If you can run one business you can run any business.
Richard Branson

Men hate those to whom they have to lie.
Victor Hugo

Part One

PROLOGUE

Nine people, once passengers, now customers, come on.

Passenger 1 Britain, yeah, beautiful country, shame we can't run a railway.

Passenger 2 This is what I feel. I feel we're doing our best, but it isn't working. That's how it feels. Every day, everywhere. Everyone's trying terribly hard. Everyone wants it to work. They have an idea what it might be like *if* it worked. People are told all the time they have to change their ways. 'It's essential we change our ways. We've got to work harder. The way we've worked is wrong.' People arrive with new schemes. But, mysteriously, things don't get better. Why not?

Passenger 1 The most basic thing you want to do anywhere is move. And in England you can't move. We're useless at it.

Passenger 4 The thing with the trains and the Labour Government is interesting, I'll tell you why. I'll tell you why it's interesting. Because the Labour Government does everything except address the problem. That's why. They did everything except address the fucking problem. They did everything except the one fucking thing they needed to do. And why wouldn't they do that? Why wouldn't they do that? Why wouldn't they do the one thing that might put everything right? Because they might get a bad review in the *Daily Mail*. I mean, think about that. Just think about it. Please.

Passenger 1 Why can the French do it? I was brought up to believe the French can't do anything. But the French can run a railway. And we can't.

Passenger 5 Man next to me, next-door neighbour in Oxfordshire, works for Warburgs, lovely house. So: Warburgs are the bank who handled the privatisation of the railways. This man made a fortune – no, I wouldn't say he made a fortune, more John Major walked him into the fucking Bank of England and said, 'Take as much as you like. Just take it.' An avalanche of money, that's what he got. Doesn't really need to, but still travels up to the City every day. The only thing he talks about? Going there, coming back? His sole topic of conversation? The state of the railways. How the trains don't run on time.

Passenger 4 I mean, take London, what about London? The whole thing of London. Ought to be a beautiful city. Why not? But nothing works. The transport doesn't work, the garbage doesn't work, the streets are filthy, there isn't a road no hole in it, and the prices are twice anywhere else in the world. Everything's here. Everything you could ever want is here, but for one thing. It doesn't work.

Passenger 1 Even I can see what to do. Even I can see it. And I've got a brain like a sparrow's nest. All shit and sticks. But even I can see what to do.

Passenger 2 We're all doing our best but it isn't working.

Passenger 4 In London, you have a tube strike and nobody gets angry. You tell me what that's about. Everyone's standing there, you can't get in to work, nobody can go to work, and nobody's upset. 'Oh yeah,' they say, 'that's how it is. That's how we are.' And it wouldn't be hard. It actually wouldn't be hard to make it work. You elect a Mayor and the Mayor does something. He does something and it all gets better. Except in his case, it doesn't. In his case he's the most popular man in London and it's all getting worse. The more roads they close, the more holes they dig, the slower the traffic, the later the tube, the dirtier the streets, the more they love Ken Livingstone. He's cheeky. You explain that. What's *that* about? You love him because he's cheeky? Everything gets worse, and you love him? For that? For *that*?

Passenger 6 What do we ask of life? That something should work. How beautiful it is when a workman arrives on time, does the job and leaves. How beautiful that is.

Passenger 7 People knock John Birt. They say he fucked up the BBC. Actually, no. I was around, I saw what happened. People can say what they like. The fact is: the BBC is now much better run. *Much* better run. It is. The programmes are worse – shame about the programmes – but the place is much better run.

Passenger 6 Why do we all want to fuck the plumber? What's the fantasy here? It's not the 1950s. There aren't people called housewives any more who sit around all day in our nighties, bored out of our minds. Not any more. But women still want to fuck plumbers. Why? Because the plumber knows what he's doing. That's why. The plumber *knows*.

Passenger 7 What did Princess Diana say? What was Diana's complaint, you remember? She lacked a business plan. 'Nobody sat me down with a piece of paper and said, "This is what is expected of you."'

Passenger 8 I've got twelve degrees, I'm an Honorary Doctor of Philosophy at Oxford University and I can't mend a plug.

Passenger 5 Britain? Yeah, well, it's nineteenth-century Russia, isn't it? And I'm not talking Tolstoy, believe me, I'm talking Gogol. Bureaucracy, inefficiency and vodka. That's what it is. Come eleven o'clock, the young men go out, they stand in the road, out on the pavement. That's it. And get their dicks out. There it is. That's how we live. Dicks out and pee in the gutter, pee the day away. For us, the Gents is too far to go.

Passenger 8 People don't like to say this. They don't like to say it, but the fact is there's something called practical intelligence, isn't there? And it's completely different – completely different – from intellectual intelligence. And I'm afraid – I'm sorry – but you pay less for it. You pay less, and that's for a reason. I could build a wall if I had to, it's not that hard, is it, to build a good wall, to make an engine, to mend a car? Be honest with me: is it that hard?

Passenger 2 We know when something is working, but no, not *how* it works – we delegate that responsibility. How the waste disappears away down the pipe, and where it goes, the alleys it travels, the path, the destination – all these are unknown to us, as our organs, our own bodies are unknown to us. A sack of mystery. We live in a paradise of ignorance, with only occasional callers to drop by, offer light and then close the door, sending us back into darkness.

Passenger 7 People die on the roads all the time, for goodness' sake. I mean, let's be honest, let's be clear, every day they die on the roads. Nobody says anything. 3,450 people die on the roads every year. But four people die on the railway and suddenly it's a crisis. And why? Because it's a symbol, that's why. The railways are a symbol. What are they a symbol of? Of national breakdown, that's what, of everything that's wrong with the country, so-called. Somebody tell me why the railways are a symbol, and the roads aren't. 3,450 isn't a crisis. Four is. Because, I tell you, as far as I'm concerned, it doesn't matter, none of it matters. Not to the person who dies. Because they die. That's what happens. That's the event. They're squashed on the road, or they're thrown into a railway cutting. What does it matter *how* they die? Why should that matter? Their death can be symbolic of the failure of the Labour Government, or it can be symbolic of the eclipse of the artisan, God knows – whatever! – it can be symbolic of Jiminy Squit – but they're still dead. That's the point. That's the point to hang on to.

Passenger 3 They didn't tell me. I said. 'Where's his shoes?' They said, 'Didn't you know? You always lose your shoes.'

Passenger 4 There's this poster everywhere. Have you seen it? Ninety-nine per cent of London Underground front-line staff have been victims of abuse. I have to say, it's a pretty impressive statistic. For a start it's way up on their punctuality rate. No one, they say, no one has the right to attack the staff of London Underground. I don't get it. I would have thought hitting the staff was one of the few remaining sources of satisfaction for the travelling public. Why can't we attack them? Why not? It's better than just standing there, waiting for the fucking train. After all: if we attacked them maybe something would change.

Passenger 3 When you're in an accident, when you're thrown from the window, didn't you know? You always lose your shoes.

Passenger 2 Everyone's got what they want. Question is – remember the song? – oh yes – how come we haven't got what we need?

Passenger 5 Tell you the problem, tell you the political problem. The problem with the railways is they're not quite important enough. Hospitals? Important. Schools? Important. They're the things governments are judged by. 'Will I die?' 'Do I know anything?' Those are real questions. 'Can I get there?' Not quite the same thing, is it? Not quite.

Passenger 6 What do managers do? Nobody knows. You know what a doctor does. You know what a carpenter does. But what does a manager do?

Passenger 9 My father always said, 'There's no free lunch.' My father was right. There's no free lunch and there's no free market. The market is rigged, the market is always rigged, and the rigging is in favour of the people who run the market. That's what the market is. It's a bent casino. The house always wins. One way or another, the taxpayer always pays for the railways. The Treasury wouldn't subsidise the railways properly when the railways were owned by the public, because they said they must be inefficient. Why? Because they were owned by the public. Now the taxpayer *still* subsidises the railways, in fact far more lavishly than ever. Why? Because they're private companies and so they must be efficient. Since privatisation, we, the taxpayers, subsidise the railways more than ever. Only now the money goes to private companies. So that's all right.

Passenger 5 Tories don't like railways. Of course they don't. They don't like buses. They don't like any form of transport you have to share. Because on a bus you might hear an opinion not your own. It spoils your world view. In a car, well, in a car, whatever you believe, there's no one to tell you otherwise.

Passenger 6 'Wanted: Marketing Manager for Sussex County Cricket Club. Interest in cricket not essential.'

Passenger 7 Do you know what we call it? When they reorganise? When they reorganise *again*? When the managers arrive and say, 'This isn't efficient, let's reorganise.' Do you know our word for it? *Bohica*.

Passenger 8 The system's stupid . . .

Passenger 7 Bend Over, Here It Comes Again.

Passenger 8 Everyone knows the present railway system is stupid. It's like trying to run a restaurant where the cooks work for one company, the waiters for another and the washers-up work for a third. With a system of fines imposed by a supervising authority if the food's inedible or the plates are dirty. That's stupid, you'd say. That's a stupid way to run a restaurant. Anyone would say. Even a moron would say, 'That's a stupid system.' And that's the system they chose.

Passenger 9 The rate of subsidy to the railways in the next five years will be precisely twice what it was when it was publicly owned.

Passenger 4 Why aren't they angry? Why aren't people angry? They were robbed. What belonged to them was taken from them by a bunch of bankers and incompetent politicians. What was theirs was given away. What was foredoomed to fail failed. And they aren't angry. Somewhere between the emotion and the belief the pedal has gone, the connection has gone. Nobody believes that by being angry, by expressing anger, anything changes, anything *can* change.

Passenger 7 'Nobody gave me a piece of paper and told me what was expected of me.'

Passenger 4 What's the point? What's the fucking point?

The Passengers go off.

Part Two

A High-Powered Treasury Thinker comes on.

High-Powered Treasury Thinker I can't imagine why you want to write a play about the railways. It's an incredibly boring subject. I'm sure, as you say, there are a lot of people eager to talk, but are they actually the kind of people you want to talk to? People who want to talk about railways are by definition nerds. If there's a play in there I'm amazed. It's so long since I even thought about them. I have to struggle now to get my mind round what actually happened. In 1991, I was one of the people running the bit of the Treasury which was concerned with what were laughingly called the public enterprises . . .

A Senior Civil Servant comes on.

Senior Civil Servant I was a civil servant at the Department of Transport from 1992 to 1997, so it was my job to help get the legislation through . . .

An Investment Banker comes on.

Investment Banker Let's think, I went into investment banking quite early in the eighties, I'd been a financial journalist and I crossed over, and somehow . . . I don't really know how it happened, somehow I became the privatisation expert in the City . . .

High-Powered Treasury Thinker British Rail at the end of the 1980s was pretty much a basket-case.

Senior Civil Servant BR was a terrible monolith . . .

Investment Banker I don't know what you'd call British Rail . . .

Senior Civil Servant The container freight department, for example, was an utter basket-case.

Investment Banker I suppose the word I'd probably use is 'basket-case'.

High-Powered Treasury Thinker I remember talking to the then-head of British Rail, man called Welsby, asking him to do something. He said, 'Look, you have to understand in this organisation the head is not necessarily connected to the rudder.' Now at that time, plainly, in the Treasury we'd grown quite arrogant about our ability to make things work better. Obviously, with privatisation, with anything, you pick off the easy things first. It's like being a fisherman, you go for the easy fish. So it was with us. Gas, electricity, phones . . .

Investment Banker My first was Singapore Airlines – '84. TSB – '85. Abbey National – '86. '87 – BA. '88 – British Steel. I got into the railways via Eurotunnel, which had to be floated in '87. People said it was unfloatable. We floated it. In fact, you can hardly get out of the country without using something I've had my fingers in, unless you fly Ryanair.

High-Powered Treasury Thinker By the time you get to the railways you're getting to the harder stuff. Thatcher's attitude had always been, 'They don't make money, let's wait till they make money and then let's privatise them.' It wasn't that she was hostile, more that – like most people – she didn't think of them as a particularly agreeable way to travel. Well, they're not. That's why only seven per cent of us use them. Nobody would choose to go on them unless they had to. I mean, would you? The one thing that was clear to the Treasury team was that we didn't want to replace a public monopoly with a private monopoly. We did that with the telephones and it didn't work. So we had the idea of splitting the track from the trains and then having competitive franchises for the actual operating companies. And then we came up with this notion called Railtrack.

Wendy comes and gives a Senior Civil Servant a cup of tea.

Senior Civil Servant Thanks awfully, Wendy.

Wendy goes as a High-Powered Treasury Thinker continues.

High-Powered Treasury Thinker I don't think, to be honest, John Major had much personal interest in it. Prime Ministers don't. He wanted to demonstrate continuity with Thatcher, but that was purely political. He used to mention them in speeches, but for the same reason he talked about invincible green suburbs and warm beer and old maids cycling to communion – he imagined if he talked about railways he would somehow connect with the British people.

Senior Civil Servant Problem: the country's run by the Treasury. Why was the Treasury in charge of transport policy? Their instinct is to try and stop everything. Always. I'll give you a for-instance. They were trying to scupper the Jubilee Line extension. Only that time one of our chaps got so furious he literally picked the Treasury chap up by his lapels, held him against the wall and said, 'If you screw this up, you little fucker, I'll see you never work in Whitehall again.' Now if you know the Civil Service, this is quite unusual.

High-Powered Treasury Thinker The Bill that went into Parliament was half-baked . . .

Senior Civil Servant I didn't personally care for the legislation . . .

High-Powered Treasury Thinker It was badly articulated.

Senior Civil Servant It's certainly not the way I would have done it . . .

High-Powered Treasury Thinker And it gave the rail regulator wide-ranging powers, and of course parliamentarians always hate that . . .

Senior Civil Servant It wasn't the policy I personally would have adopted.

High-Powered Treasury Thinker It hurts Parliament's pride to give power away.

Senior Civil Servant The Treasury model for privatisation was driven by this rather theoretical view of competition. I was in favour of twenty-five to thirty-year contracts for train-operating companies, because that way you could attract some serious long-term investment. Instead the Treasury threw the train parts in the air, crossed its fingers and offered seven-year contracts.

High-Powered Treasury Thinker So here was a piece of legislation you couldn't really explain . . .

Senior Civil Servant I'm afraid you would have to say that most of the problems of the scheme were down to Treasury ideology . . .

High-Powered Treasury Thinker . . . it really was very, very hard to explain . . .

Senior Civil Servant . . . Treasury ideology and Treasury greed.

High-Powered Treasury Thinker . . . so from the very beginning we were on the back foot and facing a lot of opposition. Having done it fast, we made two big mistakes. One: the franchises gave the train operators more interest in making money than in quality of service. Two: we didn't give Railtrack enough incentive to get the track working.

Senior Civil Servant You know, it's very hard to explain to non-Civil Service friends that you may be as deeply committed to a piece of legislation as you are convinced of its folly. Basically, yes, I was pushing through a scheme I didn't believe in. You work day and night to make a success of what you're given to do. Does that bother me? Not at all. You're a civil servant, not a politician. And the politicians? Well, Transport is oddly placed, isn't it? Ministers are either on the way up, in which case they're just using it as a ladder, or they're on the way down, and on the chilly side of the swing door, so to speak. Whichever, they're just passing through.

Investment Banker When the law was passed, then it was our job, my job, to sell the company to the City. I mean, we're not stupid people in this bank, and we thought very hard when we offered the shares at £3.90. I'd still say it was the right price. But there was a problem. The board of Railtrack didn't understand what the company was meant to be. It's there to be a trustee of engineering. That's the job. Guardian of the track. Instead, in my opinion, all the focus that should have been on the rail went onto the share. From the off, they were obsessed with share price, mesmerised by share price. And they did get it up to £17.58 in two years. And an awful lot of people did make an awful lot of money. And so then they were saying, 'Look, we're a successful company, we *must* be successful because look at our share price.' It's very easy to accuse the City of being naive. But all the City requires is a steady 12 per cent return on its money. It doesn't need fireworks.

High-Powered Treasury Thinker And then . . .

Senior Civil Servant Well then . . .

Investment Banker Then something was happening which nobody had predicted . . .

High-Powered Treasury Thinker There was a bit of bad luck.

Investment Banker Nobody *could* have predicted . . .

High-Powered Treasury Thinker There was a sudden, huge growth in the use of the railways.

Senior Civil Servant Tragic.

Investment Banker Railways were like the economy. The assumption was they would continue to decline. Instead, came this period of steady economic growth, unparalleled since the 1950s. And there was a consequent 30 per cent growth in rail usage.

Senior Civil Servant Self-evidently. Disastrous.

Investment Banker Private companies took over, they'd added some marketing sprinkle, motorways were choked to overflowing, so suddenly the thing took off. Result was, more trains. And a track, an infrastructure pushed to stress levels and beyond.

High-Powered Treasury Thinker I honestly believe things might have worked out, but when Labour got in John Prescott was put in charge. It's not a smart idea to put someone who is not sympathetic in charge of something which needs to work, because that person will not want it to succeed.

Investment Banker Prescott was deeply damaging. From the very beginning, he was riding the company. The only time I met him he said to me:

John Prescott comes on.

John Prescott 'So you're the banker.'

Investment Banker All I could think to say was, 'Yes. Sorry.'

High-Powered Treasury Thinker I think you could say, overall, of privatisation, that before Hatfield things were modestly better. Not greatly better, but a bit better.

Then came the Hatfield crash, and plainly the railways have never recovered. Since Hatfield everything is down, productivity is down disastrously. No don't ask me, I have no idea why. I'm not interested any more. All I know is: since Hatfield, something fundamental has happened and obviously all grip has been lost.

Senior Civil Servant When I left Transport, I would say the jury was out. And I haven't followed what happened since too closely.

Investment Banker When did I realise things were going wrong? Quite late. I was at our annual conference, news came that morning of one of the crashes, and then I remember someone saying, 'This division of wheel and rail ain't good.'

High-Powered Treasury Thinker Do I have any doubts about the original idea of separating track and operation? None whatsoever.

Senior Civil Servant I don't feel implicated, if that's what you're asking.

High-Powered Treasury Thinker To me it's like airports being separated from airlines. There is no inherent conflict between safety and profit. I travel by air, and if any air company became known for being unsafe it would be catastrophic for their survival and reputation.

Investment Banker I believe in the private sector. I do. I don't know if you've read Corelli Barnett's *The Lost Victory* about the 1945 Labour Government. I could only read it three pages at a time. Because it's a horror story.

High-Powered Treasury Thinker I have no regrets. I have no nostalgia for what's called the engineer's culture. In my view there were far too many engineers in the old days. It was an engineers' playground. They were always coming up with new signalling schemes which they got very excited about and which then didn't work. They needed to be managed.

Investment Banker Giving organisations to people in the public sector does seem to destroy them. I don't know about you, but I can only work when I feel the hot breath of a competitor down my neck. Otherwise, I'd be idle.

High-Powered Treasury Thinker 'The public service ethic' we hear so much about, actually it doesn't exist. Never did. I always compare it to a middle-aged man who believes he's attractive to younger women. It's a delusion.

Investment Banker I've said I don't think the basic idea was a mistake, but on the other hand I would have to admit that at every episode since privatisation, something bizarre has happened. And that does make you ask, 'Is it the structure?' It seems not fit for its purpose.

Senior Civil Servant I now watch with a layman's eye. Plainly the railway still needs billions, but unfortunately Gordon has to put everything aside for defence.

Investment Banker Do I personally feel guilty? Which answer do you want me to give? The Nuremberg defence? 'I was only obeying orders.'

Senior Civil Servant I implemented to the best of my ability policies which could have worked.

Investment Banker Or the other one? 'I didn't know what was happening.'

Senior Civil Servant I have a clear conscience.

Investment Banker I can do either. I do feel guilt. I do. But I didn't think there was anything badly enough agley that couldn't be fixed. So that's my defence.

Senior Civil Servant I love talking about the railways. My disreputable railway past.

High-Powered Treasury Thinker I've talked to you today about the railways. This is the first time I've talked about the railways for a long time. Please remember, as far as I'm concerned, this meeting never happened. It didn't happen.

A Senior Rail Executive and a Very Experienced Rail Engineer appear.

Senior Rail Executive Everyone knows: the Balkanisation was a complete disaster. The thing was broken up into 113 pieces, like beads thrown onto a table, all to be held together by local contracts and all in pursuit of the idea of competition. Well, competition on the railways is a great idea in theory, hopeless in practice.

Very Experienced Rail Engineer At one time, the Conservatives had the idea, you remember? . . .

Senior Rail Executive That's right . . .

Very Experienced Rail Engineer On the same line . . .

Senior Rail Executive Red train, green train.

Very Experienced Rail Engineer You'd have a red train leave Newcastle at nine o'clock, then a green train leave at five past. First one to the next station picks up the passengers. That's competition on the railways, all right. Just the overtaking they hadn't worked out.

Senior Rail Executive Plainly you wouldn't start from here if you were planning a railway, but given that you are here, you now have to make it work. The only people – (*His mobile rings. He gets up and walks away.*) – excuse me, I've got to take this one – who've really benefited are lawyers and accountants and consultants. (*into phone*) Hello, Derek! (*He disappears into the distance with his mobile.*)

Very Experienced Rail Engineer Privatisation gave me an opportunity because I took early retirement. I left British

Rail one weekend and started on the following Monday as a consultant.

The Senior Rail Executive returns, already talking, and sits down again.

Senior Rail Executive A lot of us who worked on the railways were keen on privatisation. We needed investment and we hated going to the government for money all the time. So it was simply a question of which mechanism. And clearly, the one they chose was the worst. It was a total and utter nonsense. When I was at British Rail, I spent one day a week getting out, meeting staff, meeting customers. Nowadays I have half the responsibility – no track, no bridges, no maintenance – all I do is run trains – and yet I struggle to get out there one day a month. Because, David, what I do now is manage contracts, monitor the contracts between all the myriad different parts of the operation.

Very Experienced Rail Engineer And you're looking at the king, remember, you're looking at the man who is king of customer care.

Senior Rail Executive Well . . .

Very Experienced Rail Engineer You're looking at the man who ran Inter-City in the 1980s.

Senior Rail Executive Bear in mind: I always say the railways are a black art as well as a science.

Sally pops in.

Sally Anyone want tea?

Both Men No, thank you.

Sally goes.

Very Experienced Rail Engineer Everybody knew privatisation was being done wrong, but politicians were determined – Rifkind, McGregor, Mawhinney who was the thug who pushed it through. The idea was, 'OK, it may not be perfect, we see it's flawed but we're not going to rethink it, so let's just see what happens. Let's see what happens.'

Senior Rail Executive The plan was, 'Throw the beads on the table . . .'

Very Experienced Rail Engineer Throw the beads on the table . . .

Senior Rail Executive 'Let's see what happens . . .'

Very Experienced Rail Engineer (*gestures*) Like that . . .

Senior Rail Executive And it's true, some will roll off, some will coalesce. We heard a lot about how the big sharks will eat the little sharks.

Very Experienced Rail Engineer All the problems stemmed from Railtrack deciding that it wasn't an engineering company, it was an access-selling company.

> *The mobile goes again. The Senior Rail Executive walks away again.*

Senior Rail Executive Me again, sorry. (*into phone*) No, it's fine, honestly, no problem . . .

Very Experienced Rail Engineer They said, 'Oh we just sell access to the railway. That's all. That's all we do.' The first Chief Executive was John Edmonds. John Christopher Paul Edmonds, to give him his full name, and he had a First in Maths at Cambridge, first-rate mind, no idiot, but for some reason he had a hang-up about engineers. He wanted to put managers in charge and shift responsibility for engineering to the private contractors. With the results we all know. He was lucky. Two weeks before the Southall train crash, Edmonds retired. He got out just in time.

> *The Senior Rail Executive returns.*

Senior Rail Executive Of course you have to subsidise railways. Always. Whatever you do. Commuter railways need subsidy because they're only used a few hours a day, like theatres. For the rest, they sit empty. You think of things like off-peak travel cards to try and fill them. I'm sure it's the same in your world. Costs have been rising dramatically and will continue to rise until Railtrack or Network Rail, as it's now called, is willing to take some risks. Because if you make a contract with an engineering company like Balfour Beatty or Jarvis to do your maintenance for you, they are going to charge a high price to indemnify themselves against risk. And ultimately we're all paying for that.

There is a silence.

Senior Rail Executive A play? You say a play? You don't think it's a book?

There is a silence.

Very Experienced Rail Engineer Most of our problems came from the House of Commons being full of lawyers. The only good Minister we ever had was Nicholas Ridley because he was a civil engineer. He knew something about what he was in charge of. Then, poor chap, he made some unwise remarks about the Germans and had to resign. People who say that at British Rail we never used to give a damn about the customer, I'd have to say they're right.

Senior Rail Executive That's why it needed a new kind of person.

Very Experienced Rail Engineer Yeah.

Senior Rail Executive The entrepreneur.

A Leading Entrepreneur comes on.

Leading Entrepreneur I took on the railways because I like a challenge, and they were an interesting challenge.

I've tried to make the whole travel experience more like an airline. More customer oriented. Just an example: I was on one of our new trains the other day, the Pendalinos, and there was no hot milk. So I rang ahead to the next station. It's details like that you have to fix. When we started the company, then it's true we were nervous of the British Rail staff, because their reputation was not great. We wanted to take them on and motivate them. So what I did was invite them to a big party at my house. I had seven thousand of them round at my place. You see, they didn't feel loved, and I wanted them to have a closer relationship with us. I wanted to give them what they hadn't had.

Obviously we would have preferred to own our own track. If 80 per cent of your trains are running late because of faulty track, then obviously you would do something about it. Under the present system all we can do is ring Network Rail and ask them to fix it. Network Rail is a seriously demoralised organisation. That's the heart of it. In life you want to be proud of what you do. People want to work for something they can be proud of. But let's face it, if you tell your friends you work for Network Rail, they are not going to say, 'That's fantastic.'

A Permanent Way Gang, all in orange, have appeared behind the Leading Entrepreneur.

Catweasel I was cutting trees one day, not far from the railway, bloke from McAlpines comes up to me, says, 'Call this number if you ever want to work on the permanent way.' You're meant to do a three-day PTS.

Rocker Personal Track Safety.

Catweasel But I never did. I just took over the name of someone else who'd done it. Let's say it's not a test I've ever heard of anyone failing.

Rustin' Hoffman There's a lot of work on the new line

22

for the Stansted Express. As much work as you want. It's all subcontracting. You don't actually know who the fuck you work for.

Doghole I work for Screwfast, believe it or not. You turn up – you're not meant to drink for eight hours – you get your hat, your hat's got your name on it, and that's the name you're known by.

The Gang all get their hats from a white cage.

Rustin' Hoffman I'm Rustin' Hoffman.

Rocker Rocker.

Big Heap Big Heap.

Catweasel Catweasel.

Sven Sven.

Stormin' Norman Stormin' Norman.

Piemuncher Piemuncher.

JH JH.

Doghole Doghole.

Rocker Could be your real name, could be not. You put on your HIVIS and you report to your PICOW – that's person in charge of work. Person in charge of machinery – PICOM.

Stormin' Norman Mile-and-a-half walk along the four-foot.

Piemuncher All tracks are the same, you got the six-foot, you got the four-foot, that's the track, then you got the eight-foot, then you got the other four-foot, then you got the six-foot again, you call that the cess.

Sven There's no danger. The only danger's tripping on the live rail. Some nights it's chaos, they send you out in the pouring fucking rain, you're meant to have a possession, you don't, you wait. There's a lot of fucking waiting, but then when you work, you fucking work. I've got a knackered tendon so I take four Neurofen a night.

JH Maybe you do one pylon, you get one pylon in before dawn. Then you walk back.

Stormin' Norman Mile and a half. Van home.

Big Heap Only one reason you're doing this. You're on £1,200 a week. You're getting home at breakfast and going to bed.

Rustin' Hoffman There is a hell of a lot of money flying about.

Big Heap A hell of a lot. And the result is it makes you mean, sort of obsessed, how little you can spend. Because there's nothing else.

Piemuncher I know one bloke eats half a Mars bar.

Doghole That's all.

Piemuncher Then at the Christmas do, the boss put £2,500 behind the bar and said to the ten of us, 'Drink your way through that.'

Doghole Didn't take us long.

A British Transport Policeman comes on.

British Transport Policeman I'd been in transport police since I was eighteen. I'm glad to hear you think it has a good reputation. I think that's because BTP always has to operate alongside other police forces, within somebody else's patch, so you've got numerically superior forces like the Met, say, working around you. That means a) you're being observed, and b) you've got someone to compare yourself with. And you have to co-operate.

When Southall happened I was at HQ. 19th September 1997. First disaster I'd ever had anything to do with. No real experience of leadership at a thing like that. First reaction was to say, 'Investigating a train crash? No, we look for rapists, robbery.' Thought: 'This is just an accident, not a CID job, not a detective's job. I'll just take down a copy of the manual for dealing with these things, that's going to be my contribution, not much beyond that.' Got in a car, got there maybe two hours after it happened, and the crime scene was very quiet, like you can't imagine. A passenger train at maximum permitted speed of 125 m.p.h. And a goods train moving across its path. And you say, OK, find out what happened.

I went into the temporary office and there was an officer from the Met, sitting with his feet up on the table. I said, 'I'm going to go down the scene.' He said, 'No, we'll go down there and report back to you.' I said to this boy, 'Take your fucking boots off the table, I'm in charge of this investigation and I'll decide who goes down there.' He said, 'Fair enough guv, got the message.' First thing I did was split responsibilities in four – dealing with the deceased, setting up the incident room, searching scene of crime for perishable evidence, then lastly dealing with the prisoner. That was the driver of the train.

Later, in the caravan, I said, 'So what's the plan for getting the deceased out of here?' They said, 'We're going to do it all in one. Wait till we've got the whole lot, then we'll take the bodies in convoy up to the mortuary for identification.' I said, 'No, identify them on the spot. If it says Jack Jones in his wallet, then let's assume that's who he is. If a bloke has a heart attack in Sainsbury's you don't seal off Sainsbury's and wait for a forensic expert. You look in his wallet and say, "It's Jack Jones, oh Christ, better go round and see Mrs Jones." So take the bodies away one by one, just as soon as you can.' They said, 'That's not what the manual says.' I said, 'I don't give a shit what the manual says. That's what we're doing.' I had a scribe, by the way, one of the first things

I did, so all my orders were written down, and we had a record of everything that happened that afternoon.

So about 5.30 I went back and I said, 'Have the bodies been removed?' They said, 'No. We're cordoning off the scene and we'll remove them all together in a group later on.' Well . . . you can imagine. There was a bloke there who was PA to the Coroner. I said, 'There are loved ones at home, wanting to know whether their family members are dead, and we are sitting on all these bodies here and that can't be right. The Coroner wants this to happen, I want it to happen, so now it's got to bloody well happen.' And then it did happen.

At the same time, the Met had set up a casualty bureau, in charge of notifying the relatives. Next day when I tried to find out why relatives weren't being notified properly, they said, 'Oh the casualty bureau is closed till 9 a.m. Monday morning.'

A Bereaved Mother and a Bereaved Father come on.

Bereaved Mother Somebody rang me up. They said, 'Put on the telly.' I looked. There was a list of the dead so-called, but there was only one name. My son's. They'd closed the office and put his name on Ceefax.

British Transport Policeman I later rewrote the manual, because nobody really had any experience of how to handle an investigation this size. Seven people killed and over a hundred injured. It was clear the driver had gone through a red light. We had a tape, terrible tape of him crying on the phone, saying, 'I've gone through a red light and I've killed lots of people.' I used to play that sometimes on police training courses, a grown man crying and screaming. It used to shut everyone up. The room would go very quiet.

But then you work on from there, David. You have to do it like an audit trail. Why did he go through the red light? Was there equipment to stop the train automatically in those circumstances? If so, was the equipment working? Was it on? Two systems in the cab, it turns out, you find out, two systems, one called AWS, not working. And the other? The most advanced train-protection system in Europe, the famous ATP, and that one? Oh I see: ATP not switched on, and, what's more, the driver not trained to use it. Why not? That's it, that's what I mean. Audit trail! You take it on backwards, from the driver, to supervisors, to management, to managing directors, and then finally to government policy, to government itself. There was no structure, you see, for investigating corporate crime. I had to make it up as I went along. A lot of the way Railtrack obstructed me. I had to go to court several times with injunctions, stuff I needed from them and from Great Western Trains which they didn't want to give me. My attitude was, this is an inquiry, don't you want to get at the truth?

Bereaved Mother Our son was referred to as Body No 6. I don't think I'd have started campaigning if they hadn't called him that.

British Transport Policeman At Southall I was accused of going native, but that's always how I've worked. It's a strength and it's a weakness. That's who I am. People say, 'Oh you were very outspoken for a policeman.' Well no, actually, I just told the truth. That's what I try to do. I mean, I tell lies like everyone else if I have to, but by and large I tell the truth. And you could say there were some jobs I might have got. You could ask, 'Why was this guy never made Chief Constable?'

Bereaved Mother I was a supervisor at Marks and Spencer's. My son Peter was twenty-nine, he worked at Freshfields, the solicitors, you know. He was a hotshot lawyer, about to be made a partner. In the firm they couldn't believe how clever he was, coming from Essex. When I heard him on the phone, I used to think, he doesn't sound like my son, he sounds like a proper lawyer. Later, when I was running the Disaster Action Group, I would find myself saying things like, 'I put it to you.' It was like he was at my side. Peter was on my shoulder.

British Transport Policeman In fact I've talked very little altogether about the whole crash.

Bereaved Mother We loved our son to bits. Very proud of him. Normal parents. On the night we were waiting to hear, we were standing in the dark, September – so the nights were getting dark already – making cups of tea and not drinking them – and we just stood in the kitchen. And I kept just saying, 'Well if he's gone, it's written,' and I felt as if this was coming from somewhere – and my husband said to me, and it was in the dark – and he'd just made another cup of tea which he'd thrown away and he said, 'Maureen' – (*to Bereaved Father*) You don't mind me saying this do you? He said, 'Maureen,' and he was crying, and he said, 'If Pete has gone you've got to forgive me.' And I said, 'What do you mean?' And he said, 'I'm not going to stay here, I'm going to go.' He was going to kill himself.

There is a silence.

Bereaved Father It's so.

British Transport Policeman I said to the team, 'We're doing this on behalf of those who died and those who are left behind. We're not doing it for any other bugger. We're doing it for them.' And then, of course, the whole thing falls into place.

Bereaved Mother We went up to the mortuary. Peter was on a trolley. His nose had come off and they'd just put it back on. And they'd combed his hair into a fringe, he'd never had a fringe in his life, and he had this fringe.

I didn't actually feel that I'd actually left my son there – because it wasn't him. His spirit had gone.

British Transport Policeman There was a point where there was going to be a railway inquiry. A railway inquiry should be subtitled 'Let's get our act together before the truth comes out.'

Bereaved Mother We've kept his room as it was, but it's not a shrine.

British Transport Policeman Then there was to be a public inquiry. And a public inquiry is only a gloss on that. Inviting people along to give their own account of what happened is bullshit. All it does is cover up. You need trained investigators.

Bereaved Mother I learnt a lot. I began to learn. Every train has an Advanced Warning System . . .

Bereaved Father It's actually a button on the floor . . .

Bereaved Mother That's it . . .

Bereaved Father . . . and when the bell goes the driver takes his foot off the button . . .

Bereaved Mother That's it . . .

Bereaved Father . . . and then puts it back on again . . .

Bereaved Mother All right, d' you mind, can I . . . d'you mind if I tell this? You see, driving a train can be quite monotonous, so every thirty seconds a driver has to prove he's still concentrating, still awake. The Swansea train had two engines; one at the front, one at the back. The train had gone down to Swansea, and in the front engine the protection system was working properly. But in the engine at the back, it wasn't working at all. It had been reported many times . . . the driver on the way down . . . many times he reported it. And that was not the first time. What you should do then – it's regular practice – you turn it round . . .

Bereaved Father You turn the train round . . .

Bereaved Mother . . . that way the engine with the working safety system is at the front. But they didn't, you see, because they would lose ten minutes.

Bereaved Father And under the privatised system, if you're ten minutes late, you have to pay a fine.

Bereaved Mother You don't know that's the reason. Not for sure.

Bereaved Father It's what I believe.

Bereaved Mother Yeah, but we're not into beliefs. We're just with the facts.

Bereaved Father Well, I've got different ideas to you.

Bereaved Mother No, we're into facts.

There is a silence.

Bereaved Father Great Western didn't want to pay the fine.

British Transport Policeman I was two years working the case. At the end, it was clear the driver was responsible, Great Western Trains was responsible, Railtrack was responsible and the Health and Safety Executive was responsible. The AWS wasn't working and it wasn't switched on. One of the few trains in the country with ATP, the best system there is, driver hadn't been trained to use it. Why not? Why wasn't it on? I studied the records, the driver records, the training records. What did I find? Great Western had cut back on training. Again: saving money. Why was the goods train going across the track? Simple. It was forty-two minutes late, and Railtrack advanced it. All right. So. We had meetings with the Crown Prosecution Service – good meetings, very good meetings, hopeful meetings. This was an avoidable incident – avoidable at every level. Here we are, it's not me, it's the CPS, there's a charge in law, it's very hard to bring, it's hard to prove, but it fits. Corporate manslaughter. We showed it to a QC, he said, 'Yes, people are ready for this. Get a good judge, this one'll stick.'

Bereaved Mother The bereaved had been told they couldn't contact each other because there was a prosecution pending. We were not allowed to talk. Not to one another. So the first time we met was at the Old Bailey.

British Transport Policeman We started with two weeks of technical discussion. At the end the judge says, 'No, there's no such charge in English law, because there's no controlling mind. To prove manslaughter you have to have a controlling mind.' And on the railways, everyone knows: there's no controlling mind. And that was it. The case fell at the first hurdle. The driver, he had his charge what they call 'set aside'. Because everyone knew. No justice in that. The driver to be prosecuted and no one else.

Bereaved Mother I'm not a rebel, I'm an M&S supervisor, you believe in people, you believe in authority.

British Transport Policeman I've never lost sleep about it. I haven't.

Bereaved Mother We were ushered into a room, and we were told.

British Transport Policeman I did feel angry that Great Western Trains and Railtrack were not made to seem as guilty as they should have been seen to be.

Bereaved Mother Everyone around the table was dumb-struck. We didn't want anyone hung or crucified. We didn't want blood and guts. All we wanted was someone to stand in the dock. That's all we expected. And we were told the law is not right for this.

British Transport Policeman Eventually Great Western were fined £1.5 million after pleading guilty to breaches of the Health and Safety at Work Act, 1974. Everyone said it was a lot but it didn't seem a lot to me.

Bereaved Mother I thought, 'This can't be right. This can't be right.'

British Transport Policeman Richard George, the Managing Director, he made three million when he sold his shares. You have to remember these are really shitty people. A lot of them just don't give a shit. Understand: I don't mean George, I'm not saying George himself. The man broke down, he cried under my questioning, though whether he was crying for himself or for others, I never really knew. I couldn't work it out. Maybe it was sadness. Or was it fear?

John Prescott comes on.

Bereaved Mother John Prescott stood in front of the cameras and he said:

John Prescott 'This must never happen again.'

British Transport Policeman I mean there was a moment with one of these managing directors when I'd needed some stuff, papers. I rang and said, 'We're coming over to get them.' The constable went over, then he rang me, he said, 'Guv, you'll never guess what's happened. I knocked on the secretary's door, said, "I'm from British Transport Police." This guy ran into his office, locked the door, and wouldn't come out.' I mean, what can you do? You have to laugh.

Bereaved Mother Later, I did an interview with one of the guys from *The Sun*. Next day they put in a two-page spread and I actually got a phone call that morning about 11 a.m. from John Prescott's office, saying would I like to meet? He gave me about an hour and a half's interview – and he had about fifteen ministers and secretaries in there with him – because he didn't really know what he was talking about – and I spoke to him specifically about the law on corporate killing and the fact that it had to change. I was a bit nervous when I went in.

Bereaved Father She's a very strong person.

Bereaved Mother I have to say – he said to me:

John Prescott 'I understand that you've been calling me names.'

Bereaved Mother And I said: 'Yes, I called you a bastard in *The Sun*.' I said, 'You've got two sons haven't you, Mr Prescott?' And he said:

John Prescott 'Do you mind if I call you Maureen?'

Bereaved Mother And I said: 'No, you can call me Maureen, but I'm going to call you Mr Prescott.' And he said:

John Prescott 'Yes, I have two sons.'

Bereaved Mother And I said, 'How would you feel, someone like yourself, if I was Minister, and I stood in front of a carriage which one of your son's bodies was lying in and obviously you thought, 'Yeah, this man's going to put it right?' And lo and behold you see nothing being done. You see a prosecution being thrown out.' And I said, 'Wouldn't you be calling me a bastard?' And he said:

John Prescott 'Yes, I would.'

Bereaved Mother I said: 'There are two train-protection systems. There's a cheap one that's no good, works with magnets, and there's a proper one they use on the Continent called ATP. It's more expensive.

There is a silence.

'We need ATP to be introduced throughout the network.'

John Prescott 'ATP will be in the next Queen's speech.'

Bereaved Mother Prescott looked at me.

John Prescott 'You're a dangerous woman.'

Bereaved Mother I said, 'I know'.

John Prescott 'And do you know why? Do you know why you're dangerous?'

Bereaved Mother 'I know why. Because I'm not paid. And I won't go away.'

There is a silence.

British Transport Policeman It all felt like a conspiracy. I don't mean like people sitting in a room, more like something impenetrable. It was in nobody's interest that the truth be discovered. Not in Great Western's, not in Railtrack's, not in the government's. I did think naively that somewhere amongst all those people that there would be someone who wanted to work in the public interest to find the truth and put it right.

Bereaved Mother Some of the bereaved, the ones who lost partners, I'm not saying this is wrong, but they have new partners. I can't get a new son. They gave us compensation. Seven and a half grand.

A Rail Union Leader comes on.

Rail Union Leader I was twenty-three years a train driver. Nothing like getting up at four in the morning and seeing all those foxes and badgers.

An Assistant General Secretary leans in.

Excuse me, the AGS just wants a word with me . . .

Assistant General Secretary Somebody's got confused between Bescott and Bedford.

Rail Union Leader You put it right then, comrade. See you tomorrow.

An Assistant General Secretary withdraws.

Mrs Thatcher nearly smashed our union. In 1999 we had debts of half a million pounds. Membership down from over 50,000 to 13,000. We've got it back up to eighteen. A Eurostar driver gets £41,000. That's top. Some drivers go as low as 23. Always the same, always goes with privatisation: a two-tier system. There's chronic low pay throughout the industry and endemic overtime factors . . .

Dawn leans in.

Dawn Have you got everything you want, luv?

Rail Union Leader Yes, Dawn. I've got everything I want. Any chance of a biscuit?

Dawn withdraws, not answering.

This is a cracked situation. It's an industry in pain. Passenger complaints are at astronomical levels. We've had all these fantastic schemes, but you have to say what exactly has been delivered? Do I know the driver? Of course. The driver at Southall? Of course. I saw him the day before yesterday. A broken man. A completely broken man. We get him up, take him out, give him a drink. He's an alcoholic now, so I suppose we shouldn't, but you have to stand by him, don't you? After all, that's what a union's for, I suppose.

A Campaigning Solicitor comes on.

Campaigning Solicitor I had a friend, a barrister actually, who died in the *Marchioness* disaster, and that's how I got into representing victims. I found myself acting eventually for fifty-one families who needed to get to the bottom of what happened, and, to be honest, the point is that I didn't give up on them when the money ran out.

British Transport Policeman Then there was this funny thing, I was actually on my way to the inquiry into the Southall . . .

Campaigning Solicitor That's the point. I didn't give up.

British Transport Policeman I was on my way in. I was on a train . . .

Campaigning Solicitor When Southall had happened in 1997, I had two clients who were passengers. What happens for a public inquiry is that the Law Society convenes a meeting of all the solicitors involved, and it happened that I was elected to represent all the passengers.

British Transport Policeman I was going to the inquiry when I heard there'd been another . . .

Campaigning Solicitor What's that film?

British Transport Policeman . . . there'd been another crash . . .

Campaigning Solicitor What's it called, that film?

British Transport Policeman . . . actually during the inquiry . . .

Campaigning Solicitor *Groundhog Day* . . .

British Transport Policeman . . . into the first crash, there was a second crash.

Campaigning Solicitor That's it. *Groundhog Day.*

British Transport Policeman And I was in the train behind.

Campaigning Solicitor It was unbelievable.

British Transport Policeman Can you believe it? This time I was in the train behind. The actual one behind. Somebody paged me, said the train up ahead had crashed. I got off the train, the Met sent a car and I said, 'Head straight for the scene.' I'd written the manual, you see. I knew more about train crashes than anyone alive. I'd spent two years. Anyway I'm driving down there, phone goes, it's the boss. He says, 'Don't go. On no account go to the scene.' I said, 'Why not?' He said, 'Let's just say: we don't want you to.' 'Why?' I said. 'Why? Give me a reason. I'm the only man who knows the procedures. Why not me? Why not? What is this? What's going on?' He said, 'We're getting a man from Leeds. He's on his way. There's a man from Leeds.'

There is a silence.

And that's how it goes.

Campaigning Solicitor I turned on the radio, I was in my kitchen. It was the 5th October 1999. The First Great Western High Speed Cheltenham Flyer had crashed head-on with a Thames train, the Bedwyn Turbo. Combined speed of 130 miles per hour. The Thames train had gone through a signal at red. We learnt later, thirty-one people had died, 533 were injured. Later, I saw John Prescott in front of the wreckage.

John Prescott 'This must never happen again.'

There is a silence.

'Money is no object in ensuring safety on the railway'.

Bereaved Father I actually would like to let it go. Since Pete's died, I just want to forget about the trains, I can't stand anything to do with trains. I would like to forget.

Bereaved Mother Even on the way out today I kissed my son's picture. There was this thing we used to say, 'Love you as big as the world.' This morning I said to my son, 'I've got to go to the National Theatre. Don't let me say anything stupid.' I'm grateful to you. You've let me come in and talk about something serious. I don't want to be gobby, I don't want to go on being gobby for the rest of my life.

British Transport Policeman Pretty soon after, I left the force.

A Young Man in Denim comes on.

Young Man in Denim My background? I had a business degree, then I was working as a distributor with the Arcadia Group, you know, Top Man and Burton's. The odd thing is I'd been in two accidents before – one in November '94 when a friend was driving and swerved to avoid a rabbit, which I wouldn't have done. I'd have driven over it.

The group was formed after the crash. It's a loose group, maybe eighty of us, maybe it's down to sixty. If you say, 'I just want to forget the whole thing,' that's fine. If you want time out, you can take it. But there's things only the survivors remember – like the smell of the scene. You don't want to describe that in any detail to strangers, but you're able to talk about it among yourselves. In fact the whole thing was very hard for a young man in his twenties to deal with. It took me a year to eighteen months to be able to talk about it at all, and that was only with the help of my psychotherapist.

I caught the train that morning from Reading. I was facing forward and I remember seeing a really good-looking girl, so I was eyeing her, in the way you do. I don't know what happened to her, I never saw her again. Anyway, there was an almighty bang. In a car accident there's only one bang, but this time there was a series and I was desperately holding on to a bar. Like being on the ferry in high seas.

I could see Carriage H was on fire. I managed to get out and I called the police from my mobile phone. Apparently I talked for seven minutes. They'd put me on speakerphone, but I couldn't answer the most basic questions. I said, 'There's been a crash,' but when they asked where, I didn't know. All I could see of Carriage H was a great wall of fire and smoke about twenty feet away. Anyway, three or four hundred of us walked across the lines, we all escaped, and even then, it's funny what goes through your head, you're nervous of stepping on a live line, or of oncoming trains. Then we all just stood there at the side of the track. It was the first time I'd seen a dead body. I'd been spared that till then. I remember a man with his suit jacket over his head. You make calculations – like there were six people already helping someone from the Thames train, so I thought, 'Oh, then they won't need me.' You want to help but you make that calculation. One man was moaning about a gash in his leg, and I could see there were people dead, so I just told him to shut up and stop complaining. Yeah.

I rang my father to turn on Sky News and Capital Radio, and then I told him I was OK and to ring the office to tell them I'd be late. The British spirit kicked in. They'd set up a place at Sainsbury's where you could get a cup of sweet tea and a biscuit. I remember asking where the Underground was. They said, 'Oh, end of the road, turn right,' and so I set off, just a slight nosebleed. When I got to work people said, 'What on earth are you doing here? I thought you were in the rail crash.' I did a day's work, and you know, I was doing well out of it, I thought, all the good-looking women in the office are loving this, then at the end of the day I bought an *Evening Standard*, saw the pictures of the crash. Obviously, the main line was closed so I went to Waterloo and went home that way – it's slower but it was OK.

I don't feel I was all there. I had this idea. Just crack on. I didn't understand the scale of the disaster. I went to the pub that evening because I felt, 'I deserve a drink, don't I?'

The first time the Reading–Paddington service was reinstated I was on that train. Very first one. It was pretty empty. And I started commuting again. It was only, I don't know, three months later I realised I was having terrible night sweats. And my neck went into spasm. Round about April, my fear of the train began to take over. I was nervous in the train, every jolt, every judder I would notice, and I could feel other people looking at me. But I still didn't put two and two together.

Of course I resisted psychotherapy. You're a young man. You think you can deal with anything. I was very suspicious. But there was a psychotherapist in the next village. And they wore me down. I gave up my job in London and got a job nearer home because I couldn't get back on a train.

I'd spoken to a friend who worked for a solicitor because I'd lost a few things in the crash – a bag with a CD player in it and some stuff like that, my nice white trainers were spoilt. They cost £90. The head of Railtrack sent us all letters, personally signed – some of us were quite impressed by that, some of us weren't – offering £1,000 in compensation plus expenses. Then the friend told me that was ridiculous. I wanted to get a solicitor onto it, but if I'm honest, I didn't like the look of . . .

Campaigning Solicitor The Ladbroke Grove disaster . . .

Young Man in Denim I didn't like the look of the one I'd seen on the telly . . .

Campaigning Solicitor The Ladbroke Grove disaster . . .

Young Man in Denim I'd seen her on the telly, I didn't care for her, she was always talking . . .

Campaigning Solicitor The Ladbroke Grove disaster is marked by a good deal of difference between two groups . . .

Young Man in Denim She's a bit of a luvvie, isn't she?

Campaigning Solicitor I'm not going to say survivors and bereaved. I'm going to say *some* of the survivors and *some* of the bereaved. Because it is true that if you lose someone . . . if you lose someone close, then sometimes you have a different attitude from someone who survives.

Young Man in Denim All that stuff about, 'Hit 'em hard, and we want people hung for this.' We didn't want to go that way. You see, the group had been formed in the first place by this woman – you know? – d'you know this woman? She became pretty well known . . .

> *A Survivors' Group Founder comes on. She wears black gloves and a plastic mask.*

Survivors' Group Founder I was in Carriage H . . .

Young Man in Denim Because of the mask . . .

Survivors' Group Founder I was conscious throughout the crash . . .

Young Man in Denim She was 'the woman in the mask'.

Survivors' Group Founder I forced myself to stay conscious . . .

Young Man in Denim She got a lot of publicity. She had the press pack after her.

Survivors' Group Founder It sounds funny to say, but my job had prepared me. I was an independent financial advisor, I advised companies, so I was trained to observe and watch and remember without having anything to write on. You daren't take notes in front of clients. It would be rude. Apart from which, it would make you seem like you didn't care. So, after the crash, I was determined to stay conscious. I took my hands down from my face, you just go on autopilot, I think. My right leg was still on fire, I didn't think anything of it, I just patted it out with my hands. And the carriage I was in, which was Coach H, had tilted on its side. And what I didn't realise, I wasn't on the outside of the crash, I was in the middle. The wreckage was wrapped right round me.

So I didn't pass out until the ambulance. Then I was three weeks unconscious in Charing Cross ICU, we were the ones not expected to make it, they'd given up on me because apparently I'd caught double pneumonia, and they thought that was curtains. Then I got moved to a National Health ward because there were some nasty viruses going around on ICU which they didn't want me to catch because of the state my lungs were in, because of the burning, and oh God, I was in hospital for three months. And so when I did come round, I didn't know anything, who'd survived, who'd died. It was sort of January before I started asking questions. Actually saying, 'What happened?' And to find out how bad it had been, and whether I was remembering right, because I'd been on drugs, not morphine, something else, I don't even know the name of it and I'd hallucinated. So yeah, really it was just a case of wanting to know if there were other people like me.

There is a silence.

Young Man in Denim That's how the group started. People just wanting to talk it over.

Survivors' Group Founder Lord Cullen asked me to give evidence. I turned up at the inquiry, and it hadn't occurred to me – the effect of the plastic mask. I hadn't stopped to think that nobody else might have it, or it might be a symbol of something. Because of course it hit every front page. It was in every single bloody paper. And I hid for five days after that.

Young Man in Denim The group was very pleased with the Cullen inquiry. Most of the survivors accept that it was a genuine accident. Because the driver went through Signal 109. Now I've seen that signal and it is hard to see in sunlight. It's true that many complaints had been made about it. I don't know, maybe Railtrack were trying to save money, or they just didn't want to do it. With my background, obviously, I see the commercial side of things. I understand their reasons. In fact the group did have a meeting with the Chief Executive of Railtrack and some of his colleagues . . .

A Managing Director of Railtrack comes on to meet a Survivors' Group Founder. They stand awkwardly together.

Managing Director of Railtrack Hello, how do you do?

Survivors' Group Founder This is . . .

Managing Director of Railtrack I'm er . . .

A Managing Director of Railtrack reaches to take her hand but does not notice it is gloved.

Oh dear.

Survivors' Group Founder It's OK. People forget. It's good of you to come.

Managing Director of Railtrack Not at all. No, no, it's very important. Very important indeed.

Young Man in Denim And people said it was very moving . . .

Managing Director of Railtrack The industry manifestly did fail on October 5th.

Young Man in Denim . . . to see great captains of industry so humbled. Very moving.

Managing Director of Railtrack We owe it to everybody who has had these ghastly experiences to talk about why, and all the things we're doing to make it better.

Young Man in Denim Sadly, I can't myself remember the meeting, because the recovery period is very grey to me.

I remember the crash and I remember recent things, but there's a period in between I'm losing. I do remember someone began to raise their voice and we all said, 'Oi, there's no need for that.' I mean, if we thumped the boss of Railtrack and gave him a good kicking, we'd not help our cause.

Survivors' Group Founder You see, there is a difference, inevitably, there is a difference between how the bereaved react to something and how a survivor reacts. I did ask a psychiatrist because the survivors' group was getting inquiries from the bereaved and to begin with I was talking to them. Then I realised they weren't on the same wavelength. When they were talking, they wanted to talk about people they had lost, which was understandable, but they almost wanted to dump their emotional baggage on you. And you sort of sat there thinking, 'Well, hang on a sec. I've been through a hell of an experience and I'm trying to come to terms with that. I don't need more emotional baggage.'

A Second Bereaved Mother comes on.

Second Bereaved Mother It was my husband's fiftieth birthday, so we were all going as a family to Portugal. My eldest son Sam was twenty-four, a mobile-phone designer, he was based in Slough, he was going down from London to clear his desk before the holiday. He went every day, with Thames Trains. We heard there'd been a crash, so we rang his mobile. He always answered his mobile, so when we got the answering machine, that's when we started to worry. We phoned the Transport Police, who were useless. They just said, 'Stay by your phone.' But they never returned our call. At 4 a.m. we rang them again, they said there's a meeting of the families at the Royal Lancaster Hotel, do you want to come along? We said, 'Yes, well, we do.'

Each family was assigned a British Transport Police person, and ours was brilliant. She said, 'There are unidentified survivors and I'm going to go to the hospital to take a look.' When she came back she said, 'They're all women.' I just howled. All over the room, I could see, policemen going to each little group, one by one, people being told individually, and the room full of howling and screaming. Then straight away some woman came up and said, 'I'm a counsellor. Do you want to talk about the death of your son?' Then I heard her on her mobile, perfectly audible, 'I'm doing some grief counselling but I've nearly finished. I'll be home soon.'

Some of the bodies couldn't be identified, so they took hair from Sam's hairbrush. That was a bad moment, because we knew the body must be destroyed, my son was totally literally destroyed. They asked us to do a DNA test, where they take a swab. The doctor doing it said, 'Someone you know well, is it?' Our policewoman, Ros, took the doctor out and I heard her screaming in the corridor outside: 'Don't you think these people have suffered enough?'

There is a silence.

Survivors' Group Founder What happened: the bereaved got angry very quickly and they wanted to kill somebody basically. They wanted a scapegoat. We kept on saying 'There is no one individual that sat down that morning and said "I know what, I'll cause that train to crash so thirty-one people will die."' We recognised it was a system failure, not a person failure. In fact, there were briefly a couple of survivors who were militant. One of their ideas was to set fire to the Chairman of Railtrack on the steps of the inquiry. They came and went very quickly because the majority of us, and by then there were eighty-one of us, weren't there? . . .

Young Man in Denim Eighty-one, eighty-two . . .

Survivors' Group Founder We were huge and we were very similar. We'd either run our own businesses, we were high up within our companies, we were directors of companies, same sort of background . . .

Young Man in Denim Sort of, good educations behind us and everything. And more sort of office workers, that sort of social group . . .

Survivors' Group Founder And wanted to be constructive as well as . . . we didn't want revenge.

Young Man in Denim It was a case of, 'Right, this has happened to us, we don't want it happening to anyone else, so let's see if we can stop it.'

Survivors' Group Founder There's nothing we could do to stop it happening to us since it's happened.

Young Man in Denim It's a bit like a case of Sod's Law. 'It's happened to us, right let's . . .'

Survivors' Group Founder Let's make sure it doesn't happen again.

Young Man in Denim Yeah, and that was the majority of us, apart from the militants . . .

Survivors' Group Founder . . . who, as I said, left.

Young Man in Denim Rather quickly, because they didn't agree with us.

Survivors' Group Founder We had a vote, we actually had a vote, whether to let the bereaved into the group.

Young Man in Denim All the facts were spelt over, all the facts were presented . . .

Survivors' Group Founder We debated.

Young Man in Denim Some people were for it, some people were against it . . .

Survivors' Group Founder And we'd always said, at the beginning of the group, even though at the time I was heading it, I said, 'This is a democratic group, you know the majority will carry the day.'

Young Man in Denim One thing I noticed, when someone said something, everyone stopped and listened attentively. It was like 'OK.' If someone didn't agree, it was like, 'I don't agree with that.' And it was not like the House of Commons where everyone shouts over . . .

Survivors' Group Founder Just different points of view. It was very civilised.

Young Man in Denim Like a debating society, really.

Survivors' Group Founder It was surprising. Two-thirds, one-third. And as the months wore on, to be honest, that third came round. It was for good logical reasons. They said, 'Yeah, we're really pleased we didn't let the bereaved in.'

There is a silence.

Second Bereaved Mother On the first anniversary of the disaster, then the survivors' group said prayers on Paddington Station with the head of Railtrack. They held a prayer meeting together. Well, you can imagine what the bereaved felt about that. The day we were due to have our memorial service, I was on the train to London, my mobile went off and it was someone watching television calling to say, 'What the hell is going on? The survivors are doing a stunt on Paddington Station.' That same time, I'd heard . . . I'd heard one of the survivors had written an article – I'm sorry this is very difficult for me – in which she was planning to say she'd woken to the smell of human barbecue. I rang her and I said, 'My son died in that crash and I've never seen him again. Please don't say that.' Next morning, the newspaper, there it was: 'I woke to the smell of human barbecue.' I'd hate to think anyone was paid for that article.

Later that day, I was in the church, you have to have a rehearsal – can you believe this? – of lighting the candles. So I'm in the church lighting candles, and I hear a voice: 'Hello, Linda. How are you?' I turn round. One of the survivors has got a TV crew. They're filming everything.

Campaigning Solicitor The train had been through a red light. It's called a SPAD. Signal Passed at Danger. Fair enough if it had been an isolated incident, but it wasn't. In what's called the Paddington throat there had been sixty-seven SPADS in six years. This particular light had been passed at danger eight times in the same period. Each time the incident reported. Each time the incident ignored.

Managing Director of Railtrack People forget: privatis-ation had been a great success. That's what nobody remembers. Punctuality was up, investment was up, the shares were at over £17.50 and 1998 was the first year since 1902 in which nobody died on the railway. True fact. That's why it annoys me when you always read, 'BR was a public asset which was given to profiteers who buggered it up.' Well, no. Actually, no. In 1998, 91 per cent of the trains were running on time. That's when Prescott called us 'a national disgrace'. People think of shareholders as young men in electric-blue shirts driving Ferraris. But they're not. Shareholders are people. They're people, like you and me. Then came Ladbroke Grove. I'm the first to admit, I made a mistake, I didn't go down there in person because we had a protocol. Because it was passengers, you see, because it was passengers who died, the protocol was: the train operating companies would go. But of course, inevitably, you can guess what happens, the operators turn up, then quietly they say to the relatives, 'Oh God, yes, Railtrack, terrible organisation, don't look after the infrastructure, quite agree.' And you appear uncaring. Which you're not. At first John Prescott was fine, he visited the site, then rang me up:

John Prescott 'We'll work together. Nobody's to blame.'

Managing Director of Railtrack Then on Wednesday, what happened, *The Sun* went for him, and on Friday the police put out a statement – completely wrong, completely misleading – saying there could be a hundred bodies, even a hundred and fifty, in Coach H, the biggest disaster since the *Titanic*. That was the problem, it took nine days to get the bodies out. Well, in the meantime all hell broke loose. Alastair Campbell got nervous and on Saturday afternoon, too late for me to respond, he briefed the press, saying Railtrack were villains and that the government was putting in inspectors to review safety procedures. I will say this for Campbell: when Downing Street briefs, they do a professional job. I rang John Prescott. I said 'Do you know what you're doing? This is the safest form of transport there is. The most dangerous part of a train journey is the walk to the station. And the British system is one of the safest in the world, and now you're accusing us of killing people.' He told me he was a politician, I'll never forget it, he said:

John Prescott 'If you go, you get a pay-off. If I go, I get nothing.'

Managing Director of Railtrack Can you believe that? Do you believe it?

There is a silence. Then Lord Cullen enters. Everyone becomes the Cullen inquiry.

Lord Cullen Good morning. I've been authorised by the Attorney-General to conduct a public inquiry into the cause of the death of thirty-one persons on October 5th 1999. I shall start by reading the terms of reference of my inquiry. 'To inquire into and draw lessons from the accident near Paddington Station . . .'

Lord Cullen goes on mouthing his terms of reference under:

Second Bereaved Mother The Cullen inquiry was a catalogue of shame. It was a complete cover-up.

Managing Director of Railtrack The Cullen inquiry was a medieval witch-hunt.

There is a hiss.

I was hissed at whenever I got up to speak.

Second Bereaved Mother From the start Cullen gave everyone immunity, and so we thought, 'Oh, this is wonderful, they'll be free to tell the truth without fear of prosecution.' What actually happened was they didn't need to disclose anything. I thought, this is the Mad Hatter's Tea Party. These people have been promised that whatever they say – whatever – say what they like and no harm will come to them. And *still* we don't have the truth.

Managing Director of Railtrack People in Railtrack uniforms were spat at in newspaper shops. We needed a new chairman and 147 people turned the job down. The *Socialist Worker* put up six hundred pictures of me all over the Underground. The caption read: 'Wanted for Serial Killing.' My mother used to close her eyes, and only open them between stations.

Second Bereaved Mother The truth is, a lot of the time they forget you're there, they behave as if you're not there. It's very English, David. Like the famous moment when the head of Railtrack said:

Managing Director of Railtrack 'The pursuit of safety is a journey and you never arrive at your destination.'

More hissing.

Second Bereaved Mother How could he say that unless he'd completely forgotten who was in the room? I just burst into tears. I mean, his appearance at the inquiry was very emotional for all of us. When the Managing Director stepped up:

Lord Cullen Your name, please.

A Protester Judas!

Second Bereaved Mother And then, just after, as he turned to speak, another man took off his shirt. Underneath, he'd hand-printed a T-shirt: 'You murdered my daughter.' One of us followed him down the street and said, 'Look in my eyes and tell me you're sorry.' The Railtrack boss issued a statement:

Managing Director of Railtrack 'My wife has been very upset.'

Second Bereaved Mother Well, we were pretty upset ourselves.

At this a group of Bereaved Parents unfurl photographs of their dead children.

Lord Cullen This inquiry understands and appreciates that the feelings of the bereaved and their families are indeed the subject of this inquiry – we never forget that – but it is very hard for witnesses to testify when photographs of the dead are displayed directly in front of them. I am therefore suggesting the photographs be moved to a table I have designated for this purpose.

The Bereaved Parents go into a huddle. Their Spokesperson answers.

Spokesperson The families agree to put their photographs on a table, but they do not agree to the table being at the side of the room. The table must be at the centre of the room.

There is a pause.

Lord Cullen Move the table.

Second Bereaved Mother Whenever we got too close to anything, Cullen would say:

Lord Cullen 'Let's not go down that route. This is an inquiry, not a court of law.'

Second Bereaved Mother And I wanted to say, 'Yes, but it's your job to get at the truth. You're meant to be the professional, you're meant to test what people are saying, and to point out when it doesn't make sense.' But he didn't. That's why we used to call out 'Rubbish!'

A Protester Nonsense!

Second Bereaved Mother Just so somebody did. One of the lawyers referred to Ladbroke Grove as an 'accident'.

A Protester Disaster!

Second Bereaved Mother I saw the lawyer going red.

Lord Cullen Yes, yes, disaster . . .

Second Bereaved Mother Next day we sent Cullen the *Oxford English Dictionary* definition of the word 'accident'. We all did. Because Ladbroke Grove wasn't an accident. In the signal box, they admitted, there's an over-ride button you can push and straight away you close down the whole Paddington throat. But of course they don't. They never touch it. My guess is they don't want to delay the Heathrow Express. My view, they only seem to have two rules on the railway: never delay the Heathrow Express, it's the golden cash cow; and the second is: don't kill tourists.

They tried to blame the driver for everything, because . . . the obvious reason: he was dead. First, they claimed he was on the phone. Then it turned out he didn't even have a mobile phone. Now his widow has been in touch, she was very nervous about asking whether she could come to our meetings. She was worried she wouldn't be welcome among the bereaved. I hope she'll come. I told her: 'You're just as much a victim as us.'

Young Man in Denim I believe the Cullen report was a good thing and we can work to make lights safer.

Second Bereaved Mother I can see they would like us to go away. *The Times* called us – was it safety fascists or safety Nazis? I can't remember. We turn up at the meetings with the reports under our arms, and we have them all marked, with particular points to raise and places to question, and they all go, 'Oh no, they've actually read it. They've actually read the report.' What they resent most is that we're not the hysterical bereaved, we're the informed bereaved.

Young Man in Denim I've got a new girlfriend now, but I'm what they call between jobs. I've settled for £18,000. Of course part of you thinks, maybe that isn't as much as I might have got. But part of you thinks, great, eighteen thousand, pay off the debts, pay off the credit card, buy a car. I went to Oldham about a Citroen Xara, second hand. I've been on the German motorways with it. I got it up to 145 m.p.h. Fantastic! Going downhill, and with the revs just touching red. It's wonderful to pass a police car at 110. Incredible! I love risk. But I've quietened down from five years ago. I'm less cocky. Then if someone cut me up, I used to get out, bang on their window: 'Do you know what you've done?' Now, I let it go.

Second Bereaved Mother When Concorde crashed, every family got a million pounds. In one swoop, they got the whole issue out of the way. It's not the money, it's just so you don't ever have to think about it. The bereaved from Ladbroke Grove are still forced to argue. Three and a half years later we're going to meetings to establish what they call VOL – Value of Life. Each child, they say, has a different value, maybe ten thousand pounds, maybe twenty. The other day, to establish the value of Sam's life – the value of Sam – they asked me, 'How much did he spend on Christmas presents?' How does it make a parent feel to be told that because his son is a road sweeper his life is worth less than a brain surgeon?

Campaigning Solicitor If you lose children, you become very committed. You might think that losing a partner would be the thing, but in my experience it isn't so. It's losing an adult child.

Young Man in Denim My attitude is: we can do something here, so let's do it. Let's keep our drive and enthusiasm to keep going. The Paddington Survivors' Group is a very strong brand and image.

Second Bereaved Mother The bereaved don't need to be a group. We all share the same grief, so you see we've never needed to formalise anything. There is no leader. There is no structure. You're bound by something far deeper than a name, or an organisation. By understanding what each has been through and by needing to know why.

Campaigning Solicitor The bereaved know what they want. They want to know that what they have been through will not happen again, and that somebody will be held accountable. These two things.

Second Bereaved Mother In all this my views are the views of most ordinary people and nobody is articulating our views. I suppose I didn't hold any strong views before Sam died. I had brought my children up to believe there is right and wrong, but there was no political theme in my life. You have this faith that people are good and honest, but then you meet politicians. We have met powerful people we would not otherwise have met. In yourself you have tremendous strength, you have a strength because nothing in life can ever be as bad as that day. And you see very clearly that there is a political game going on, particularly with this government. To them people are unimportant. Because they are holding on to power. It's the only thing for them. And that power has corrupted them.

Young Man in Denim I like being here. In the pub. Solid chair, solid ground. I feel safe. When I get jumpy again, then I get in the car and drive round with some nice music on. That calms me down.

There is a silence, then a Scottish Literary Editor comes on.

Scottish Literary Editor I wrote about Hatfield because I lived down the road from it. Of course if you talk about the railways, you tend to be written off as a trainspotter. It's a love affair. It's something men do when they don't have women. Railways are very peculiar, very special. Think about it. All that weight, all this huge mass of metal travelling along a contact point something like a sixpence. Something very powerful, isn't there, in the imagination? The worst image of Auschwitz – that tragic little terminus under the gate. Not far from Hatfield is a stretch of track . . .

Campaigning Solicitor It's like that film . . .

Scottish Literary Editor . . . known as Howe Dell . . .

Campaigning Solicitor What's that film?

Second Bereaved Mother There's a pattern, isn't there?

Scottish Literary Editor . . . a curve that trains have safely negotiated for a hundred and fifty years. At 12.23 on October 17th 2000, just one year after Ladbroke Grove . . .

Campaigning Solicitor What's the name of that film?

Second Bereaved Mother It's a pattern.

Campaigning Solicitor What is it? What's it called? What's the name of that film?

Second Bereaved Mother The pattern goes: Rail accident. Inquiry. Recommendation. No action. Rail accident. Inquiry. Recommendation. No action.

Senior Rail Executive Hatfield? Well, what can you say?

Scottish Literary Editor . . . the 12.10 King's Cross to Leeds express entered the curve at 115 miles per hour – the maximum permitted speed for that stretch of track – and came off the rails. The rail shattered into three hundred pieces – like a bicycle crushing a biscuit. The accident did what even the war had failed to do – it brought Britain's railways to a halt. 450 tons of train exerted pressure on a rail that had been known to be faulty for over eight months.

Campaigning Solicitor *Groundhog Day.*

Senior Rail Executive Hatfield proved what we all knew – that Railtrack was out of control. What happened would simply not have happened under British Rail. It wouldn't have happened. Not in the British Rail days.

Another Senior Operating Executive comes on.

Another Senior Operating Executive I can tell you exactly what happened to me on the day of the Hatfield crash. We were going to a training meeting at Bolton Abbey, and when I heard there was a crash, as Managing Director of the operating company, I just thought, 'Oh Christ.' I knew I had to get to York as fast as possible. I phoned Nick Pollard of Railtrack, and he said, 'I've got the helicopter.' All the time I was thinking, 'Oh Christ, is this our crash?' You see, GNER had had a wheel-break some months earlier at Sandy. I was thinking, 'Oh God, if this is a wheel-break, then no question, it's five years down the pan.' And remember at the time we were competing to renew our franchise. So I knew: 'If this is our fault, that's the end for GNER.'

The helicopter with Nick was the worst forty-five minutes of my life, in a bubble, in the air, unable to do anything. There was a real chance we might be arrested when we got there. I was thinking, 'Jeepers! It really could happen!' When we got there, the first thing Nick and I did was go to the hedge. We were desperate for a pee. The security services were there, because there was a chance it was a bomb. The police were furious, because they wanted first access to the scene. And meanwhile the media were buzzing like bees. I knew very well that if it was our accident, then we'd have to pull our whole fleet.

About nine o'clock a policeman came by. He said, 'Don't think it's anything for you to worry about. It's a broken rail.' And my God! My God! I thought, 'Thank Christ it's not us.'

A Vicar of Hatfield comes on.

Vicar of Hatfield I'd only been here a month. At the time of the crash. But we'd already had meetings. After September 11th, we were forming teams to deal with disasters. I was actually driving away from the town, because the Church of England is changing its liturgy and I needed to go on a training course in Watford. It took me two hours to get back. The whole town was shut down. We'd agreed in advance that in the case of a disaster, our involvement should be on an 'if you're asked for' basis, so I didn't go down to the site. Because they didn't ask for me.

Another Senior Operating Executive We've learnt from Hatfield. Now we have a dedicated disaster room. We have rehearsals. In fact when that man drove his car at Great Heck near Selby over a bridge and onto our line – complete freak, freak accident – the press were already there. I went down the line straight away, saying, 'This is a car accident, it's not a train accident, this is it, this is what we're doing bang bang bang.' Next morning at

York, I tell you, very moving, huge amount of hugging. All the drivers were hugging each other. Even I got quite emotional. I've never been hugged by so many people in my life. I saw the railway for what it is. A big family.

Vicar of Hatfield On the Sunday after, we had an open church, we thought the survivors and bereaved might like to come, but in fact it was mostly the town. People want spiritual comfort and that's the facility we offer. Contrary to what people think, a lot of churches are full. The head of Railtrack came and lit a candle. He's a brave and compassionate man. Everything that happened was at a great human cost to him and his wife. That gets forgotten. He's a good Christian man. So our main job as Christians was to keep the media away from him.

My own view is that we've got the balance wrong between the human and profit. Privatisation has introduced the element of greed. We're all so used to looking for individual satisfaction, we've forgotten the group. There is a drive for self-fulfilment, not for fulfilment with each other. We are not a happy people. They introduced profit versus expedience versus safety. It's in every industry, not just rail. Competition seemed to be a good idea but . . .

Strange thing, I remember a few years ago, I was on a pilgrimage from Winchester to Canterbury, burning hot summer's day, I was with my father. By the roadside we came across this gang of railway workers, brewing up a cup of tea by the side of the road, skiving I suppose. Brewing, anyway. We had a cup of tea with them. They said, 'All this cost-cutting is going to hurt, a major accident is inevitable.' They foresaw it. It was a very vivid experience. It was prophetic.

I feel my job is to defend Hatfield's name. The way the town is labelled. It's a byword. Like Slough. Hatfield equals crash equals tragedy. We've been struggling to not be tarred, not with negative, nasty, nasty, nasty labels.

Here we have all the problems of terrible unemployment, the disenfranchised. To value the places that are being slagged off, it's a very Christian thing to do. Jesus values that that is least valued. I like to remind people: Hatfield is a place with people in it.

Christianity is a religion of hope. We live in a society obsessed with blame, with blaming each other. As a nation we've lost our confidence, and so we have some kind of need to make someone accountable. There seems to be no acknowledgement of human frailty. Did you see the Paxman interview with Tony Blair? People were being so rude. The man is doing his best. This rudeness, this terrible rudeness all the time – 'It's his fault!' – it's always someone else's fault – this obsession with blame, it debases us, it degrades us.

David, I would like to see a drama of people who make things work. If Hatfield is in a play, I'd like it to be mentioned as a town of determined people. The town will regenerate and rebuild up and rise up out of all this.

A Technical Director of a Maintenance Company comes on.

Technical Director I can tell you about the rail. I'm technical director of Jarvis, and we took over maintenance of that stretch of track after the accident. So I actually have a piece of that very rail in this office. Look – honey-combed right through.

Scottish Literary Editor When Hatfield happened, they came upon this thing called gauge-corner cracking – which was actually something engineers had known about for fifty years, but which was suddenly on everyone's lips – as if they had any idea what they were talking about.

Technical Director It should have been ground down, that's what you do, but you need a special machine. Spinorail had it. The only country to have the track-grinder was Spain. We have one now but it's still not approved.

Scottish Literary Editor I put the collapse of morale down to basic disproportion. Say you're working on the railways and you earn £16,000, £18,000, and yet you know that the lawyers and bankers walked away with literally billions of pounds – well it's bound to make you cynical, isn't it ? You could, crudely, be loyal to British Rail – just. How can you be loyal to Stagecoach

Technical Director People say, oh, it's all sub-contracting nowadays. And that's bad, they say, because so much can go wrong. Well: we do outsource. We do. But not the important jobs. Not management jobs. We sub-contract labour. I mean, we're not hiring brain surgeons. They're shovel pilots. Some of them can't even read and write, but by Christ they can shovel ballast.

A Managing Director of Railtrack returns.

Managing Director of Railtrack Straight after Hatfield I offered to resign.

Scottish Literary Editor The chief executive did actually offer to resign.

Managing Director of Railtrack It was our fault. The condition of the track was appalling, it was totally unacceptable. The rail was scheduled to be renewed, there was a series of local cock-ups, someone ordered the wrong kind of rail. The track had been ultrasonically tested in June, and the ultrasonic tester didn't work. Speed restrictions should have been put on. Yes. Of course. And they weren't. And so I was working on the Carrington principle: the buck stops here. Next morning, in bed, quarter to six, the phone goes, it's John Prescott waking me up, calling from a banquet in China:

John Prescott 'What bloody happened?'

Managing Director of Railtrack I gave him the good news that I was resigning. I went in, started packing my desk. Then people began calling, which was nice. The operating companies. The survivors' group. And even the politicians, because when they thought about it, they didn't like the idea, not because I was wonderful. No, they liked me because I took all the crap. They thought, 'Who'll get the flak? Shit, if the chief executive goes, there won't be anyone to take the flak.' They needed me as air cover. So I was persuaded to stay.

First thing I did was close down large parts of the network. Looking back, sure, it was too big a reaction, I know that, but we had no choice. Ladbroke Grove had made it inevitable. The engineers were back in charge. In all that search, we didn't find one rail in the condition of Hatfield. It's easy to put on speed restrictions, but with all the Health and Safety rules it's much harder to get them lifted. Two weeks later, I realised we were running far too slowly over perfectly safe pieces of track.

Of course, last thing I was thinking about during all this was my non-execs. You don't. Why would you? Non-execs are peculiar people at the best of times, always looking out for their own position. Lot of them can't even hold their knives and forks properly. Anyway, they decided. I still don't know why. I heard the phrase 'lance the boil'.

There is a silence.

The enemy is always in the seats behind you.

Scottish Literary Editor When the chief executive was sacked, three weeks after Hatfield, Railtrack was left in the hands of two forty-three-year-olds who had less than a year's experience in running a railway between them.

Managing Director of Railtrack We got a super press the day I left.

Scottish Literary Editor On November 27th the peace-time record for the slowest ever railway journey was set on the 10 p.m. express from London to Nottingham which finally arrived at 7 a.m. – nine hours to cover 126 miles. The chief executive was replaced by a man whose experience was in the financial department of Yorkshire Water, and who now makes cardboard boxes in Bedfordshire. Until Hatfield, the word 'engineering' had never appeared on Railtrack's floor plan.

Managing Director of Railtrack You learn a lot about yourself and fall back on yourself and who you are and how you were brought up. All that rubbish. Actually it isn't rubbish. That's what I learnt. Overall, we felt we'd behaved in a way where we could live with ourselves. It may not be easy and I might have made my fair share of mistakes, but there is something more meaningful about a public service job than there is about flogging Smirnoff vodka. Besides, someone has to do it.

There is a silence.

Scottish Literary Editor On May 10th 2002, the 12.45 from King's Cross to King's Lynn was ten minutes into its journey, travelling at 80 m.p.h., when it derailed and smashed into the station at Potter's Bar. A fractured lock stretcher bar caused the points to fail catastrophically. The nuts from the bar were found lying at the side of the track. Nobody has yet taken responsibility for the failure of maintenance.

A Squadron Leader comes on.

Squadron Leader Got onto the train, elected to sit in First Class, not something I usually do. Then two people got on . . .

A Bereaved Widow comes on.

. . . and one of them asked me:

Bereaved Widow 'Is this the train to Cambridge?'

Squadron Leader Said I was fairly sure it was, and if it wasn't, we could share a cab as we were all going to the wrong place together. Those were the only words we spoke. Train set off. Steward came along, started at our end – I thought, 'This is all going really good.' Had myself a whisky. The two people I later found out were Nina and Austen had a drink. I remember Austen debating whether he should have a beer or not, and Nina said:

Bereaved Widow 'Oh go on, have a beer, we're on our holidays . . .'

Squadron Leader Unless you've been derailed, you probably can't imagine, you're bouncing along the sleepers, so you're doing this – (*Gestures.*) – and I thought, 'I know what happens here, we glide to a halt, swear at British Rail, climb out and wait for the next train.' I must stress that all these kinds of thoughts, you think them at the time, but they're instant. You think a lot quicker than you can speak. So then I looked across and saw Nina really bouncing up and down in her seat – really hitting her legs under the table – and I looked at Austen, I thought, 'What are they jumping up and down for?' Then I realised I was doing exactly the same thing. I thought, 'Oh crikey, this is a bit interesting,' and then the carriage tilted away from me, the carriage flipped to its side, I was whisked out my seat, I was horizontal above the seats with my head in direction of travel. It was like being in a tumble dryer. It really was. My next memory was seeing Austen go past me, again with his arms and legs flailing – big man, heavily built chap – and I thought, I don't want to get tangled with him, big flailing limbs and stuff, that could hurt. So I grabbed a little hand rail, I didn't see what it was – there's something! I'll hold on to that – as it turned out, for grim death. The carriage was debris and dust, and your vision was gradually closing down. From the moment we flicked onto the side my memory goes into black and white. I don't have a coloured memory, and they reckon it was probably because the brain was getting so busy, it was maxing out, it said, 'Cut the colour channel, let's worry about the other stuff, a black-and-white memory is just fine for what you're about to see, lad.'

We were doing 100 miles an hour when we came off the track, so it was bounce, bounce, bounce – bang onto the side – skid through ninety degrees – take out the bridge. Up onto the platform. Bang. Ten seconds, probably. Quite a violent stop because I remember thinking, 'Ah, that's it. I'm dead.'

There is a silence.

Scottish Literary Editor One thing you can say – it's incredible but you can say, if you look at Potter's Bar – no apology. No prosecution. No admission of liability. No proper compensation. No inquiry. The fourth crash – and in the response, the worst of the lot.

There is a silence.

Squadron Leader I lay there. I thought, 'Crikey. I'm alive. But I'm not a happy teddy bear.'

Bereaved Widow I have no memory of anything about the crash. Apparently a Squadron Leader got me out from under the seat . . .

Squadron Leader As you know, Nina is built like a sparrow, so I lifted her out. Put her on some cushions, horizontally. Propped her head up.

Bereaved Widow . . . but I have no memory of it. I've met the Squadron Leader once.

Squadron Leader I've met Nina twice. Once conscious. Once unconscious.

Bereaved Widow I was scared to meet because of the memories it might stir. I knew about him because he contacted the hospital in Barnet to see how I was doing. He told me that Austen died instantly, so that is some mercy to know. Railtrack have not admitted responsibility because they were told by Jarvis, who were responsible for the maintenance of the line, that there was 'compelling evidence of sabotage'. Needless to say, no such evidence has ever been produced and the Health and Safety Executive has dismissed such an explanation.

We had a press conference. I worried that I'd be ill, that I wouldn't be able to cope, but when I got there I surprised myself with my own anger. I remember seeing a lovely older woman – well, I shouldn't say older because I'm old myself. A little old lady, and she's lost her grand-daughter. There's a lovely Nigerian lady left with four kids under fourteen. We went to see Railtrack one afternoon. They're incredibly skilled with what they call the victims. It's not nice to be called a victim. At one point one of the men was smiling, no doubt being pleasant. I said to him, 'You can take that smirk off your face.' And he did. What did we hope for? There are three things we want. A handsome sum for everyone injured and bereaved, a proper apology, and vertical integration.

I never believed in corruption before. I'm not talking about greased palms, or bribes. I'm talking about the idea of corruption, it being in everyone's interest – the politicians, Railtrack, Jarvis – to do nothing. The response of ordinary people is very different. A group of friends were in a cab travelling to Austen's memorial service, and the driver remarked on the bells pealing out over Trafalgar Square. When he was told they were ringing for someone killed in the Potter's Bar crash, the cab driver turned off his meter. He said, 'It's the least I can do.'

They know, you see. People know.

The problem with the system is that everyone is able to pass the buck and nobody feels any responsibility.

Meanwhile Jarvis, including that evil man Steve Norris, have got the contracts for the Northern, Piccadilly and Jubilee lines. So they're doing fine.

What makes me angriest is the waiting. The waiting makes me angry. You want someone to say sorry, and that way release you from what happened. But until they say sorry you can't put it behind you.

I once read of a woman who wrote a letter to her friend, mourning her dead husband. She sought for comfort and could find none anywhere. 'Except,' she said at the end of her letter, 'there is one thing. I shall have more closet space.' And that is about the sum of it.

We were together for forty-eight years. My lover, my friend.

I find the pain easier to deal with when I'm talking about it. I haven't really been able to go back to work. I was one-third of the way through a children's book. I've picked it up once and looked at it, but it belongs to another world.

There is a silence.

Scottish Literary Editor Just nine months ago, on February 5th 2003, Alistair Darling stood up in the House of Commons to explain the government's new policy on ATP. This is the Europe-wide safety system which John Prescott made many firm promises to introduce and for which the relatives of the dead of all four crashes have been campaigning. The government has decided to abandon the targets for its introduction. On June 24th the contractors Jarvis announced record profits for the year following the Potter's Bar crash.

The stage clears.

Part Three

EPILOGUE

Everyone reassembles.

Scottish Literary Editor What it comes down to is, they don't want to spend the money. They haven't the guts to stop private companies bleeding money out of the system, and they haven't the will to take control. The railways will never be renationalised. I'm not optimistic. Someone said, tarmac the lines over. Make them motorways.

Leading Entrepreneur Of course it's been concerning, all the knocking that's gone on in the last five years, but the service hasn't been as bad as you might think. Do people differentiate between problems caused by Railtrack and problems caused by the operator ? Of course they don't. (*Laughs.*) We were very concerned it would affect our brand. But research shows we've held up remarkably well. Virgin is still Number One most-trusted brand among men, and Number Three among women. What's One and Two? Oh, er, let me think, Boot's definitely and . . . I'm not sure. Marks and Spencer's?

Scottish Literary Editor You see, the train-operating companies don't even own their own trains. The banks own the trains. And they rent them. Did you know that? You didn't, did you?

Managing Director of Railtrack It is the most amazing story, but now I'm getting on with my life, ha ha. I lay doggo for a few months and then I was parachuted into Woolworth's. The whole thing was negative in a business sense, hugely positive in a human sense. On my CV I have a three-year gap with nothing on it. I don't mention the railway. Harvard Business School, yes. Blue chip companies, yes. The railways, no. I learnt a huge amount but it wasn't what you'd call career-enhancing. In my world, being in charge of the railways is not a plus. I'm forty-eight, I'm chairman of a big company and ideally I'd like to pick up another one, be chairman of a second. I think you can say that Business Britain does not want people on boards more famous than they are. And the reaction to my name is still *Mein Gott! Mein Gott!*

Leading Entrepreneur There was never a lot of money to be made. As it turned out, there isn't going to be money made out of the railways. The odd thing is: it's going to return to being a public service, which is what it's always been. Only run by business people. We're going to be doing it because we believe in it. To have someone whose reputation is on the line, who can be identified – like me – is going to be a good thing. I don't think anyone's going to be doing it for the money.

Survivors' Group Founder The group has shrunk. I mean, quite a few have wandered off, wanted to start afresh. Perfectly understandable. There've been some went back to work, a bit like, went back to work, thought they could cope. Couldn't. So had to come back again. When I set up the group I remember one of the first things I said was, 'This group will have been successful when it no longer has any members.'

There is a silence.

I need a break actually. Sorry, my concentration has just gone 'ping'.

Scottish Literary Editor To be honest, I don't think the English are good at the communal. It's not their gift. For instance, look, they're hopeless at cities. The English idea of paradise is to go away at weekends, keep hounds and live in Bicester. It's as if we don't want fully to commit to the notion of living together.

68

Another Senior Operating Executive I have a marvellous job. Marvellous. I look out at six o'clock. If the station's full of people not going anywhere, you say, 'Oh Christ! Shit!' If they're moving you say, 'Yippee!'

Scottish Literary Editor The truth is that nowadays governments want to shed responsibility. The whole move is to put yourself in a situation where you are not responsible – nobody can blame you. That's why the government will never take the railways back. The only things governments now like to have are standing armies, navies and air forces, because those you can boss around. You tell them to do something, they do it. 'Go fight that war.' Off they go. It's a simple relationship.

Squadron Leader I'm trained to fly Tornadoes and that's what I went to do. We had two pilots go down from the base. It's war, not fun and games, and in war you lose people. I don't lose sleep at night because I fought in the Iraq war.

Young Man in Denim I feel now the anniversary is for the bereaved. First year, I went to the memorial service and it was a mistake. It wasn't for me. Soon as it was over I said to my dad, 'We're out of here.' I spend the day of the anniversary in bed. Get up at 5 p.m. I wanted to have a party this year to say, 'Yes. I've survived.' The bereaved can't do that. I feel very guilty for surviving. I feel very guilty.

Bereaved Mother Peter got away from work early. He actually ran for the train – they held the train for him. I mean, this is funny. I believe it was written.

Squadron Leader I was back in time for the anniversary service on Potter's Bar station. Incredible, but they're still not admitting it was sloppy maintenance. Nobody's said 'sorry'. That sticks. Nina's the public side of things.

She's got fantastic spirit. They're trying to wear her down. They'd love it if she died.

Second Bereaved Mother You know, perhaps all this isn't going to achieve anything, but you keep going. You go on. Our son . . . our son would not put anything down, he had this thing, David – he didn't get it from me – he was persistent, he saw things through. If there was a puzzle he kept going till he solved it and got it perfect. You have to understand, after twenty-four years of bringing your son up, you don't stop loving him. You don't stop just because he dies. You still want to do things for him. You need to find out why.

Bereaved Widow I've coined a phrase for what we feel. Those of us who've been through these ordeals. I call it hysterical friendship.